Preparing for the SHRM-SCP® Exam 2026/27

Third Edition

Preparing for the SHRM-SCP® Exam 2026/27

The Official Workbook and Practice Questions from SHRM

Third Edition

Editors: Charles Glover, MS, Director,
Certification and Assessment Products, SHRM,
and Hanna Evans, MPS, SHRM-CP, Manager,
HR Certification and Assessment Products, SHRM

First published in the United States and Great Britain in 2026 by Kogan Page Limited

Society for Human Resources Management (SHRM)
SHRM, Alexandria, Virginia, shrm.org
SHRM, India Office, Mumbai, India, shrm.org/in
SHRM, Middle East and North Africa Office, Dubai, UAE, shrm.org/mena

Kogan Page
Kogan Page Ltd., 2nd Floor, 45 Gee Street, London EC1V 3RS, United Kingdom
Kogan Page Inc., 8 W 38th Street, Suite 902, New York, NY 10018, USA
www.koganpage.com

EU Representative (GPSR)
eucomply OÜ, Pärnu mnt 139b–14 11317, Tallinn, Estonia
www.eucompliancepartner.com

Kogan Page books are printed on paper from sustainable forests.

ISBNs
Paperback 9781398627796
Ebook 9781398627802

Library of Congress Cataloguing-in-Publication Data
A CIP record for this book is available from the Library of Congress.

British Library Cataloguing-in-Publication Data
A CIP record for this book is available from the British Library.

Typeset by Hong Kong FIVE Workshop, Hong Kong

Contents

APPENDIX 1

APPENDIX 2

Acknowledgments

This workbook was made possible by the thoughtful and generous advice, guidance, and input of many smart and talented subject matter experts, especially the following:

Mike Aitken, Executive vice president, members and communities, SHRM

Alexander Alonso, PhD, SHRM-SCP, chief knowledge officer, SHRM

Nicholas Schacht, SHRM-SCP, product development and events, SHRM

Nancy Woolever, MAIS, SHRM-SCP, vice president, academic and student communities, SHRM

Sarah Chuon, SHRM-CP, specialist, exam development, SHRM

Giselle Calliste, SHRM-CP, specialist, exam development, SHRM

Jasmine Bell, SHRM-CP, specialist, exam development, SHRM

Sampoorna Nandi, PhD, sr specialist, certification and assessment products, SHRM

We also gratefully acknowledge the scores of SHRM members, SHRM certificate holders, and exam candidates who provided input for this book.

Introduction

We applaud your decision to move your career in Human Resources forward by pursuing a certification with SHRM! To this end, this workbook is designed to help you prepare for the **SHRM Senior Certified Professional (SHRM-SCP®)** exam.

Specifically, the SHRM Senior Certified Professional (SHRM-SCP) designation is for HR professionals who are relatively advanced in their careers. This level of professional primarily works in a strategic role, such as developing policies and strategies, overseeing the execution of integrated HR operations, directing the entire HR enterprise, and leading the alignment of HR strategies to organizational goal, and much more. The SHRM-SCP exam is designed to test this *strategic*-level HR knowledge and proficiency.

In this third edition, we continue to place emphasis on utilizing and understanding the SHRM Body of Applied Skills and Knowledge (SHRM BASK®)—bridging the knowledge, concepts, and competencies that the SHRM BASK encapsulates to the SHRM-SCP exams. Perhaps most importantly, this workbook includes a total of 70 practice items that were used on past SHRM-SCP exams. These practice items will provide you with more exposure to the types of items that you will see on the real exam, as well as feedback about correct responses. These items were not simply created for this book—they were taken from actual SHRM-SCP exams that were used in previous years.

On the other hand, the SHRM-CP exam is designed to determine who has the level of competency and knowledge that is expected for HR professionals who perform (or will perform) operational work. This includes such duties as implementing policies, serving as the HR point of contact, and performing day-to-day HR functions. Although the SHRM-CP and SHRM-SCP exams are very similar in structure, this workbook is focused exclusively on the SHRM-SCP exam.

It is important to note that this workbook is designed to be used along with the official SHRM study guide: *Ace Your SHRM Certification Exam: The Official SHRM Study Guide for the SHRM-CP and SHRM-SCP Exams*, the SHRM BASK, the SHRM Certification Exam Preview app, and the SHRM Certification Prep System®. The study guide includes much additional information about the exam and exam preparation strategies, and it also includes a set of practice items from a combination of the SHRM-CP and SHRM-SCP exams. The SHRM BASK reflects the blueprint for the SHRM-SCP exam and should be used to develop your study plan. The SHRM Certification Exam Preview app is an additional resource for SHRM practice test questions that are broken down by the competencies listed in the SHRM BASK; it is a tool specifically designed to guide you to make the best application decision possible by getting a realistic preview of the two different exams so you apply for the exam that matches the type of work you do. Choosing the right exam to take is the most important decision you will make. The SHRM Certification Prep System is the comprehensive preparation tool offered by SHRM built upon the SHRM BASK.

In this SHRM-SCP workbook, some of the key concepts that were introduced in the study guide are further explained. For example, a self-assessment for gauging strengths and development areas that are addressed in the exam was briefly introduced in the study guide; this is created in the current workbook to help with SHRM-SCP exam preparation.

Thank you for allowing SHRM to embark on this journey with you toward SHRM-SCP certification and beyond!

How to Apply

SHRM offers both certification exams during two testing windows every year. The first window is from May 1 to July 15, and the second window is from December 1 to February 15. Examinees choose where to take the exam in person at one of more than 500 Prometric testing centers across more than 180 countries.

After you have decided which exam to take, apply to take the exam on the SHRM website anytime between the Applications Accepted Starting Date and the Standard Application Deadline.

Examinees who apply by the **Early-Bird Application Deadline** and/or who are **SHRM members** receive a reduced exam fee. Note that exam applications apply to specific testing windows; after you have applied, transferring to the next testing window incurs an additional fee.

To learn more about the benefits of SHRM memberships, receive discounts on the SHRM Certification Prep System and the SHRM Certification exams, and much more, navigate to this link: https://www. shrm.org/membership.

To apply, you must:

1. Apply online (https://www.shrm.org/credentials/certification).
2. Create a user account.
3. Select the exam level you are eligible to take.
4. Complete the application form by agreeing to follow the terms of the SHRM Certification Candidate Agreement.
5. Pay the application fee.
6. After you receive your Authorization-to-Test (ATT) letter, schedule your exam directly through SHRM's test delivery vendor (https://www.prometric.com/shrm). Your ATT letter will outline several ways to schedule your exam and select your testing location.

ONLINE
Learn More about How to Apply for the Exam

https://www.shrm.org/credentials/certification/how-to-get-shrm-certified-process

SHRM-CP and SHRM-SCP Eligibility

SHRM Certified Professional (SHRM-CP)

- The SHRM-CP certification is intended for individuals who perform general HR or HR-related duties, or for currently enrolled students and individuals pursuing a career in Human Resource Management.
- Candidates for the SHRM-CP certification are not required to hold an HR title and do not need a degree or previous HR experience to apply; however, a basic working knowledge of HR practices and principles or a degree from an Academically Aligned program is recommended.
- The SHRM-CP exam is designed to assess the competency level of HR at the operational level. This level includes implementing policies, supporting day-to-day HR functions, or serving as an HR point of contact for staff and stakeholders.
- Refer to the SHRM BASK for detailed information on proficiency standards for this credential (i.e., Proficiency Indicators only for All HR Professionals).

SHRM Senior Certified Professional (SHRM-SCP)

- The SHRM-SCP certification is for individuals who have a work history of at least **three years performing strategic level HR or HR-related duties,** or for SHRM-CP credential holders who have held the credential for at least three years and are working in, or are in the process of transitioning to, a strategic level role.
- Candidates for the SHRM-SCP certification are not required to hold an HR title and do not need a degree to apply.
- The SHRM-SCP exam is designed to assess the competency level of those who engage in HR work at the strategic level. Work at this level includes duties such as developing HR policies and/or procedures, overseeing the execution of integrated HR operations, directing an entire HR enterprise, or leading the alignment of HR strategies to organizational goals.
- Applicants must be able to demonstrate that they devoted at least 1,000 hours per calendar year (Jan.–Dec.) to strategic-level HR or HR-related work.
    - More than 1,000 hours in a calendar year does not equate to more than one year of experience.
    - Part-time work qualifies as long as the 1,000-hour per calendar year standard is met.
    - Experience may be either salaried or hourly.
- Individuals who are HR consultants may demonstrate qualifying experience through the HR or HR-related duties they perform for their clients. Contracted hours must meet the 1,000-hour standard.
- Refer to the SHRM BASK for detailed information on proficiency standards for this credential (i.e., Proficiency Indicators for All HR Professionals and for Advanced HR Professionals).

Who Should Take the SHRM-CP® vs SHRM-SCP® Exam?

To help professionals—including those who are HR accountable for people management and organizational outcomes—determine which SHRM certification aligns with their career stage and responsibilities, it is essential to understand the target audience for each exam. Below is a comprehensive breakdown of job titles and professional profiles suited for the **SHRM-SCP® (Senior Certified Professional)** certification.

SHRM-SCP® (Senior Certified Professional)

The **SHRM-SCP®** is intended for senior HR professionals who operate at a strategic level, influencing organizational direction, leading HR teams, and driving complex HR initiatives. This certification is best suited for those who:

- Are mid- to senior-level HR professionals.
- Lead HR functions or departments.
- Develop and execute strategic HR initiatives.
- Influence organizational policy and decision-making.
- Manage complex and multi-faceted HR projects.

Job Title	Example Responsibilities	SHRM BASK Functional Area(s)	SHRM BASK Behavioral Competencies
HR Manager/ Director	Develops and executes HR strategy, oversees HR programs, manages HR staff, ensures compliance	HR Strategy, Organizational Effectiveness & Development, Risk Management	Leadership & Navigation, Business Acumen
Senior HR Business Partner	Advises business leaders, aligns HR strategy with business objectives, manages complex employee relations	HR Strategy, Employee & Labor Relations, Organizational Effectiveness & Development	Consultation, Business Acumen, Leadership & Navigation
HR Consultant	Provides expert HR advice, leads organizational change projects, develops HR solutions for clients	Organizational Effectiveness & Development, Risk Management, Talent Acquisition	Consultation, Analytical Aptitude
HR VP / CHRO	Sets HR vision, leads HR strategy at executive level, influences C-suite decisions, oversees all HR functions	HR Strategy, Corporate Social Responsibility, Managing a Global Workforce	Leadership, Business Acumen, Ethical Practice

Job Title	Example Responsibilities	SHRM BASK Functional Area(s)	SHRM BASK Behavioral Competencies
Director of Talent Acquisition	Develops and executes talent acquisition strategies, manages recruiting teams, oversees employer branding	Talent Acquisition, Organizational Effectiveness & Development	Leadership & Navigation, Consultation, Inclusive Mindset
Compensation & Benefits Manager	Designs compensation strategy, oversees benefits programs, ensures market competitiveness	Total Rewards, Technology Management	Analytical Aptitude, Business Acumen
Global HR Manager	Manages HR across multiple countries, ensures global compliance, leads international HR projects	Managing a Global Workforce, Corporate Social Responsibility	Business Acumen, Inclusive Mindset
HR Operations Manager	Oversees HR systems, optimizes HR processes, manages compliance and reporting	HR Function Structure, Technology Management	Analytical Aptitude, Leadership & Navigation
Senior Learning & Development Manager	Designs enterprise learning strategy, manages leadership development, evaluates training effectiveness	Learning & Development, Organizational Effectiveness & Development	Leadership & Navigation, Consultation, Analytical Aptitude

Actionable Guidance

- » Identify your strategic responsibilities to match them with the SHRM BASK® functional areas and competencies above.
- » Focus SHRM-SCP® exam preparation on areas where you drive organizational impact, lead teams, and advise senior leaders.
- » Use your experience in strategic HR initiatives to contextualize exam scenarios and apply advanced concepts.

By connecting your senior HR responsibilities to the SHRM BASK, your exam preparation is both strategic and relevant, positioning you as a leader and change agent.

If you believe the scope of your experience and responsibilities do not meet those outlined above, we recommend consulting the SHRM-CP Workbook and reviewing the SHRM-CP Certification Exam Previews. SHRM Certification Exam Previews offer unique practice question sets to assess your readiness for either the SHRM-CP, SHRM-SCP, or a mixture to enhance your readiness and confidence ahead of test day. Whether you are looking for half-length exams or content domain specific offerings to enhance your areas of opportunity, SHRM is committed to your success, ensuring you have the tools to pick the exam that is right for you.

SHRM-CP® (Certified Professional)

The **SHRM-CP** is designed for HR professionals who are primarily engaged in operational roles, focusing on the implementation of policies, day-to-day HR functions, and supporting organizational HR initiatives. This certification is ideal for those who:

» Are early to mid-career HR professionals.

» Have responsibilities centered on policy implementation, transactional HR activities, and employee relations.

» Are building foundational HR expertise and competencies.

Section 1

The SHRM-SCP Exam Structure

Types of Exam Items

As defined in the *Ace Your SHRM Certification Exam* study guide, and on the SHRM website, there are two general types of items on the SHRM-SCP exam: (1) knowledge items (KIs) and foundational knowledge items (FKIs); and (2) situational judgment items (SJIs).

Knowledge items (including FKIs) are stand-alone multiple-choice items with four response options. Each KI tests a single piece of knowledge or application of knowledge.

Situational judgment items (SJIs) present realistic situations from workplaces throughout the world. Based on the scenario presented, SJIs ask test takers to consider the problem presented in the question within the context of the situation, and then select the best course of action to take. As with the KIs, these are multiple-choice items with four response options.

The distribution of items with respect to content and item type is essentially the same for both the SHRM-SCP and SHRM-CP exams. About half of the items on each exam are allocated across the three behavioral competency clusters, and the other half are allocated across the three HR knowledge domains. Approximately 40% of the items on each exam are situational judgment items, and the remainder are stand-alone items measuring either knowledge that is foundational to the behavioral competencies (10%) or HR-specific knowledge (50%).

Item Type	
Situational Judgment (40%) Foundational Knowledge (10%)	HR-Specific Knowledge (50%)
Behavioral Competency Clusters	**HR Knowledge Domains**
Leadership (19%) Business (17.5%) Interpersonal (13.5%)	People (19%) Organization (18%) Workplace (13%)

Exam Items

The SHRM-SCP exam consists of a total of 134 questions—110 of the questions are scored, and 24 of the questions are unscored. The purpose of unscored items is to gather data to determine if they are viable to become scored test items on future SHRM exams if they perform well. Think of unscored items like beta testing to gather tester data. While unscored items will not affect your overall score (getting unscored items incorrect will not count against you), it is important not to skip any questions.

The scored and unscored items are intermingled throughout the exam and are indiscernible from one another. This exam is broken into two equal halves, and each half contains 67 questions.

Each half is divided into three sections:

» **Section 1**: 20 KIs and FKIs (i.e., knowledge items for behavioral competencies)

» **Section 2**: 27 SJIs

» **Section 3**: 20 KIs and FKIs

Exam Timing

The total exam appointment time is four hours, which includes **3 hours and 40 minutes** of testing time for the exam itself. This equals approximately 98 seconds per question. It is important to use your time wisely.

It is critical to note that you will be unable to return to Exam Half 1 upon moving to Exam Half 2. Ensure that you have answered all of the questions to the best of your ability in Exam Half 1 before proceeding to the second half of the exam. There will be confirmatory prompts for you before transitioning to Exam Half 2.

The exam time is broken down into the following segments:

» **Introduction**, including agreeing to follow the terms of the Candidate Agreement and confidentiality reminders: 4 minutes

» **Tutorial**: 9 minutes

» **Exam Half 1**: Up to 1 hour and 50 minutes

» **Exam Half 2**: Up to 1 hour and 50 minutes

» **Post Exam Survey**: 6 minutes

There are a few transition screens throughout the exam that account for the remaining minutes.

Key Takeaway	Details & Guidance
Types of Exam Items	• The exam features **Knowledge Items (KIs & FKIs)** and **Situational Judgment Items (SJIs)**, both are multiple-choice with four options
Item Distribution	• **~40% SJIs** • **~10% foundational knowledge items** • **~50% HR-specific knowledge items**; split between behavioral competencies and HR domains

Total Questions & Scoring	• **134 questions total:**
	  • **110 scored**
	  • **24 unscored** (used for future exam development; indistinguishable from scored items)

Exam Structure	• **Two halves** (67 questions each), each half has:
	  • 20 KIs/FKIs
	  • 27 SJIs
	  • 20 KIs/FKIs

Time Management	• **4 hours total**
	  • **3 hours 40 minutes** for exam; **20 minutes** for intro/tutorial/survey
	  • **~98 seconds per question**

No Return Policy	• Once you move to **Exam Half 2**, you **cannot return** to Exam Half 1 • Confirm all answers before proceeding
Scored & Unscored Items Mixed	• **Scored and unscored items are intermingled** and **indiscernible**; answer all questions as if they count

Section 2

The SHRM BASK

One of the most important things for you to understand as you prepare for the SHRM-SCP exam is this:

> **All of the HR competencies and knowledge areas that are assessed on the SHRM-SCP exam are detailed in the SHRM BASK.**

Conceptually, preparing for the SHRM-SCP exam is not unlike preparing for the SHRM-CP exam. Do not be fooled, however, they are completely different exams by design, emphasizing differences found in the **proficiency indicators** area of the SHRM BASK. You may be tempted to rely on your professional experience as preparation. Alternatively, if you have taken the SHRM-CP, rely on your preparation and knowledge gained to carry you through the SHRM-SCP exam. It is critical to match your knowledge and experience with the key concepts and proficiency indicators with those in the SHRM BASK for **Advanced HR Professionals** ensuring you feel comfortable and confident with the material. If not, the SHRM-CP may be the best place to begin your journey until you are ready to elevate your credentials.

The SHRM BASK can also be thought of as the blueprint for the SHRM-SCP exam, much like an architect uses a blueprint to construct a building, testing programs use an 'exam blueprint' to build examinations. You can find the complete version of the SHRM BASK at:

> https://www.shrm.org/credentials/certification/exam-preparation/body-of-applied-skills-and-knowledge

While the SHRM-CP and SHRM-SCP share the same exam blueprint, the exams are designed to be completely distinct by way of using proficiency indicators to separate the knowledge, skills, and abilities required to address *operational-level* (SHRM-CP) HR duties and tasks versus *strategic-level* (SHRM-SCP) HR functions and responsibilities.

Important reminders as you prepare for the SHRM-SCP exam:

» If something is not covered in the SHRM BASK, it is not eligible to be tested on the SHRM-SCP exam. However, the SHRM BASK is an expansive document that covers many different areas, and given its breadth, you might not see everything that is presented in the SHRM BASK represented on the SHRM-SCP exam in any given testing window.

» The SHRM BASK does not define your specific HR role, but rather the HR professional role in general. Therefore, it may cover more than your current or past HR roles.

» For individuals testing outside of the US, you are not held accountable for content covered in the US Employment Law & Regulations section of the SHRM BASK (Workplace content domain). Those items will be substituted with items from the Workplace domain.

Figure 2.1. The SHRM BASK Model

This workbook is designed to demystify the SHRM BASK, providing insights to aid your test preparation using the SHRM BASK as a study tool. In this section, we provide guidance on how to break the SHRM BASK into digestible segments to help you identify areas of strength and areas that you need to study more, ultimately creating a personalized study plan in preparation for the SHRM-SCP exam.

Structure of the SHRM BASK

Simply reading through the SHRM BASK may be a daunting task due to the amount of information it contains. Before tackling the detail, it can be helpful to understand the structure and the elements comprising the model. Let's start with the basics.

» HR technical competency; divided into three content domains: *People*, *Organization*, and *Workplace*.

» Behavioral competency; divided into three content clusters: *Business*, *Interpersonal*, and *Leadership*.

The HR technical competency, **HR Expertise**, reflects the technical knowledge specific to the HR field for an HR professional to perform their role. **Behavioral competencies**, on the other hand, describe the knowledge, skills, abilities and other characteristics (KSAOs) that define proficient performance for a professional. They are more general in their applicability than the profession-specific technical competency. That is, many of these competencies may apply to different jobs, roles, and professions but have been specifically defined in HR terms for the SHRM BASK.

In short, the HR Expertise technical competencies reflect what knowledge HR professionals apply on the job, and behavioral competencies reflect how they apply this knowledge.

Before we dig deeper, Figure 2.2 presents a high-level overview of the SHRM BASK structure including how Key Concepts (KC) or Proficiency Indicators (PI), or both, support the content area you are studying. Ensure you review the applicable Key Concepts and Proficiency Indicators, where applicable.

HR Expertise		
People	**Organization**	**Workplace**
» HR Strategy [KC/PI] » Talent Acquisition [KC/PI] » Employee Engagement & Retention [KC/PI] » Learning & Development [KC/PI] » Total Rewards [KC/PI]	» Structure of the HR Function [KC/PI] » Organizational Effectiveness & Development [KC/PI] » Workforce Management [KC/PI] » Employee & Labor Relations [KC/PI] » Technology Management [KC/PI]	» Managing a Global Workforce [KC/PI] » Risk Management [KC/PI] » Corporate Social Responsibility [KC/PI] » **US Employment Law & Regulations* [KC/PI]

Behavioral Competencies			
Leadership	**Leadership & Navigation** [KC]	**Ethical Practice** [KC]	**Inclusive Mindset** [KC]
	» Navigating the Organization [PI] » Vision [PI] » Managing HR Initiatives [PI] » Influence [PI]	» Personal Integrity [PI] » Professional Integrity [PI] » Ethical Agent [PI]	» Connecting I&D to Organizational Performance [PI] » Building the Infrastructure for an Inclusive and Diverse Culture [PI] » Ensuring Impartiality & Fairness [PI] » Cultivating an Inclusive and Diverse Culture [PI] » Operating in a Global Environment [PI]
Interpersonal	**Relationship Management** [KC]	**Communication** [KC]	
	» Networking [PI] » Relationship Building [PI] » Teamwork [PI] » Negotiation [PI] » Conflict Management [PI]	» Delivering messages [PI] » Exchanging Organizational Information [PI] » Listening [PI]	
Business	**Business Acumen** [KC]	**Consultation** [KC]	**Analytical Aptitude** [KC]
	» Business and Competitive Awareness [PI] » Business Analysis [PI] » Strategic Alignment [PI]	» Evaluating Business Challenges [PI] » Designing HR Solutions [PI] » Advising on HR Solutions [PI] » Change Management [PI] » Service Excellence [PI]	» Data Advocate [PI] » Data Gathering [PI] » Data Analysis [PI] » Evidence-Based Decision-Making [PI]

** US Employment Law & Regulations content will only appear if you are testing within the US If you are testing elsewhere across the globe, those items will be substituted with other items from the Workplace HR Expertise domain.*

Figure 2.2. Overall Structure of the SHRM BASK

HR Expertise

The HR technical competency, HR Expertise, reflects the principles, practices, and functions of effective HR management. This competency is grouped into three main knowledge domains: *People, Organization, and Workplace*. The knowledge domains are further divided into 14 HR functional knowledge areas that describe the technical knowledge required to perform key HR activities.

- **People:** HR Strategy, Talent Acquisition, Employee Engagement & Retention, Learning & Development, and Total Rewards
- **Organization:** Structure of the HR Function, Organizational Effectiveness & Development, Workforce Management, Employee & Labor Relations, and Technology Management
- **Workplace:** Managing a Global Workforce, Risk Management, Corporate Social Responsibility, and US Law & Regulations

Each HR technical competency includes the following information:

- Definition of the functional area.
- Key concepts describing the knowledge specific to the functional area.
- Proficiency indicators that apply to **All HR Professionals** (i.e., early career through executive career levels) as well as those that apply primarily to **Advanced HR Professionals** (i.e., senior and executive career levels).
    - Note that for the SHRM-SCP, proficiency indicators for Advanced HR Professionals are the key ones to attend to.

Behavioral Competencies

Behavioral competencies facilitate the application of technical knowledge. Successful HR professionals must understand and effectively perform the behavioral components of HR practice in addition to being in command of technical HR knowledge. The eight behavioral competencies are grouped into three clusters:

- **Business**: Business Acumen, Consultation, and Analytical Aptitude
- **Interpersonal**: Relationship Management and Communication
- **Leadership**: Leadership & Navigation, Ethical Practice, and Inclusive Mindset

Unlike the HR technical competency, each behavioral competency is further comprised of 3 to 5 sub-competencies for a total of 31 sub-competencies. Refer back to Figure 2.2 for an overview of the sub-competencies by their competency and cluster. For each behavioral competency, the following information is provided:

- Definition of the competency.
- Key concepts describing the foundational knowledge for the competency.
- Sub-competencies applicable to the competency, with definitions.
- Proficiency indicators that apply to all HR Professionals as well as those that apply primarily to advanced HR professionals.
  - Similarly, proficiency indicators for Advanced HR professionals are the key ones to attend to when preparing for the SHRM-SCP exam.

Key Concepts and Proficiency Indicators

Structural Difference in the SHRM BASK

In addition to the what and how distinction between HR Expertise and behavioral competencies, another difference important to understanding the structure of the SHRM BASK focuses on where the key concepts and proficiency indicators are specified in the model.

As depicted in Figure 2.2, key concepts (KC) and proficiency indicators (PI) are specified for each knowledge area under **HR Expertise** technical competency (note the superscripts beside each knowledge area). However, behavioral competencies are structured differently in this regard: Key concepts are identified by behavioral competency, and proficiency indicators are identified by sub-competency.

The SHRM-CP certification focuses on the proficiency indicators identified for *All HR Professionals*, and the SHRM-SCP certification exam focuses only on the indicators identified for *Advanced HR Professionals*. Although the proficiency indicators relevant to all HR professionals clearly apply to advanced HR professionals at the senior and executive levels, they are not assessed directly on these indicators but are expected, on the job, to understand the concepts behind these functions, recognize their strategic importance, and be able to mentor junior employees in developing those behaviors.

Example of Parallel Proficiency Indicators

An example of this distinction can be seen by parallel proficiency indicators presented under the *Corporate Social Responsibility* (CSR) knowledge area within the Workplace functional knowledge domain.

- For **Advanced HR Professionals**: *Develops a CSR strategy that reflects the organization's mission and values.*
- For **All HR Professionals**: *Identifies and promotes opportunities for HR and the organization to engage in CSR activities that align with the organization's CSR strategy.*

Both proficiency indicators address the organization's CSR strategy. The *advanced* proficiency indicator highlights the higher-level organizational focus of developing this strategy, whereas the *all* proficiency indicator focuses on supporting the strategy by identifying and promoting opportunities in alignment with the organizational strategy.

How to Use the SHRM BASK for Studying

Now that you have an understanding of the overall structure of the SHRM BASK, the next step is to understand the format of exam items and how you can leverage the information in the SHRM BASK to help your preparation for the exam.

Item Types

Both the SHRM-CP and SHRM-SCP certification exams consist of two types of items: knowledge items (KIs)[1] and situational judgment items (SJIs).

Knowledge Items

KIs are stand-alone, multiple-choice items that test a single piece of knowledge or application of knowledge and make up 60% of the exam. Topics stem from the key concepts and proficiency indicators presented throughout the SHRM BASK.

Each KI assesses content knowledge according to one of four possible cognitive classifications, or levels of understanding or application, required to answer it:

» **Recall** items test the facts for that key concept such as defining a specific term or identifying a component of a theoretical model. This is the most basic type of KI.

» **Understanding** items requires the test taker to demonstrate their content knowledge by comprehending information, comparing two things, translating by applying knowledge or interpreting a concept to apply it to an example. These items assess the test taker's ability to recognize how HR concepts and terms manifest themselves in the workplace.

» **Problem-solving** items require test takers to apply their knowledge to develop a solution to a problem, which is something HR professionals do every day. To select the correct answer, the test taker must draw on their knowledge and understanding of many different concepts and strategies, which is more cognitively demanding than simply recalling the information.

» **Critical evaluation** items ask test takers to analyze information to predict an outcome. A competent HR professional uses the ability to predict outcomes to guide business strategy and execution.

Situational Judgment Items

In comparison, SJIs test decision-making and judgment skills to identify the most effective response according to HR best practices, as established by HR subject matter experts. These items make up 40% of the exam, and involve three major components:

1 The *Ace Your SHRM Certification Exam: The Official SHRM Study Guide for the SHRM-CP and SHRM-SCP Exams* references two types of knowledge items: KIs and foundational KIs (FKIs). KIs and FKIs follow the same structure; the only meaningful difference is that the content for a KI stem from a knowledge area under *HR Expertise*, whereas the content for an FKI stem from a *behavioral competency*. For this workbook, we refer to all knowledge items as KIs.

- A realistic situation (scenario) that is similar to what many HR professionals have likely experienced during their careers.
- Two to three questions addressing the scenario prompting test takers to solve a particular situation-specific issue in an action-oriented way.
- Four possible response options.

For example, while a KI may test your knowledge about different communication elements or techniques (for example, under the *Communication* behavioral competency), an SJI may ask you to identify the most effective way to communicate with leaders or with the organization given the circumstances presented in the scenario. In lieu of being able to assess each test taker's real-life response to the same situation, an SJI offers an opportunity for test takers to leverage their knowledge of key concepts, as well as HR best practices, to demonstrate how they might have responded to a similar real-life situation.

For more information about these item types, please refer to the SHRM Certification Prep System or *Ace Your SHRM Certification Exam.*

Creating a Study Plan from the SHRM BASK

As noted previously, simply reading the SHRM BASK all at once may be overwhelming and, as a result, not particularly helpful as a test preparation approach. Rather, the model needs to be consumed in smaller quantities. In the remainder of this section, we present an approach to examining the different components of the SHRM BASK to identify particular topics to study and further investigate during your test preparation.

First, we recommend picking a knowledge area or behavioral competency and sub-competency as a starting point. From there, you will leverage the key concepts and proficiency indicators to support the development of your customized study plan. You will repeat these steps for each knowledge area and sub-competency until you have completed your review of the SHRM BASK.

We present examples of applying this approach to a knowledge area and a behavioral competency and sub-competency in Section 3.

How to Study Key Concepts

Key concepts are the most straightforward component of the SHRM BASK with respect to identifying information to build your study plan. They specify the complete list of topics that will be covered on both the SHRM-CP and SHRM-SCP exams. Figuring out what you need to know and what is tested on the exam is an excellent place to start.

How to Study Proficiency Indicators

Proficiency indicators are a bit more complicated to use for building a study plan. They require more self-reflection and analysis than key concepts. As noted previously, proficiency indicators reflect what competent HR behavior and performance look like in practice. That is, they define high-level HR best practices according to their associated knowledge area or behavioral sub-competency. We present some recommended steps to analyze a proficiency indicator to help build your study plan.

Before we get started, you need to be clear which exam you are preparing for: SHRM-CP or SHRM-SCP. Remember that proficiency indicators are differentiated by which exam you will take. Indicators for all HR professionals will be assessed on the SHRM-CP exam, whereas indicators for advanced HR professionals, as well as all HR professionals, will be assessed on the SHRM-SCP exam.

Important Reminder

When reviewing the SHRM BASK, it is important to remember that the competency model reflects expectations for the HR profession in general and not your specific HR role or those of others in your organization. It is easy to get confused about what you do (or have done) in your career and what is considered proficient for the HR professional at your level in general.

Depending on your current job and past experiences, you may not have had the opportunity to perform or experience everything specified in the SHRM BASK, and that is okay. You don't have to have experience in all the areas presented to be eligible to take the exam. They are a guide as to what is expected of an HR professional at your level.

QUICK TIP
Recommended Steps to Identifying Key Concepts to Study

1. Review the list of key concepts for the particular functional knowledge area or behavioral competency of interest.
2. Ask yourself the following questions:
   » Which concepts do I know extremely well?
   » Which concepts am I only familiar with at a superficial level?
   » Which concepts do I have limited to no knowledge about?
3. Take note of with which key concepts you have only some or no familiarity. These are good targets to add to your study plan. It can also be useful to refresh on the key concepts that you think you know extremely well.
4. Think about how the key concept could be tested with KIs, according to the four cognitive levels (i.e., recall, understanding, problem-solving, and critical evaluation).
   » What are the facts about this key concept?
   » How would I demonstrate understanding of this key concept?
   » What types of problems could I be expected to solve that would rely on this key concept?
   » Can I predict outcomes under varying conditions?

QUICK TIP
Recommended Steps to Understanding Proficiency Indicators for the SHRM-SCP exam

1. Review the proficiency indicators for *Advanced HR Professionals* for a particular knowledge area or behavioral sub-competency of interest.
2. Ask yourself the following questions:
   » Which indicators resonate with experiences I have had during my HR career?
   » Which indicators am I familiar with because I have observed others perform them?
   » Which indicators am I unfamiliar with altogether?
3. As you did with the key concepts, take note of which proficiency indicators fall into each category. They will all require some further analysis to support your test preparation.
4. For each proficiency indicator, think about which key concepts are valuable for supporting the proficient performance of this indicator. Linking key concepts to proficiency indicators can aid your understanding of different applications for a key concept and scenarios you could encounter on the exam in KIs and SJIs.
5. For each proficiency indicator, identify the HR best practices for this indicator.
   » Think about what steps are involved in satisfying the proficiency indicator.
   » Identify any additional key concepts that you didn't initially select that could now be useful to study more closely. Go back to the recommended steps for using key concepts to determine if these need to go on your study plan list.
   » Consider that you may know the ways that you have handled this proficiency indicator in the past and these responses may have been effective for your given situation, but they may not actually reflect HR best practices.
   » Take note of the situations you have encountered or witnessed that have involved this proficiency indicator as these could be reflected on the exam.
   » Identify and add any HR best practices and proficiency indicators to your study plan list.
   » Can I predict outcomes under varying conditions?

Key Takeaway	Details & Guidance
SHRM BASK Is the Exam Blueprint	All HR competencies and knowledge areas tested on the SHRM-SCP exam are **detailed in the SHRM BASK**. If a topic is not in the SHRM BASK, it is not eligible for testing.
Strategic vs. Operational Focus	While SHRM-CP and SHRM-SCP share the same blueprint, **proficiency indicators** distinguish operational (CP) from strategic (SCP) HR responsibilities. Prepare for advanced, strategic-level scenarios for SHRM-SCP.
Structure: Technical & Behavioral	The SHRM BASK is divided into **HR Technical Competencies** (People, Organization, Workplace) and **Behavioral Competencies** (Business, Interpersonal, Leadership). Each domain contains specific knowledge areas and sub-competencies.
Key Concepts & Proficiency Indicators	Every area is supported by **Key Concepts (KC)** and **Proficiency Indicators (PI)**. For SHRM-SCP, focus on indicators for Advanced HR Professionals. These drive both knowledge and application questions on the exam.
Not Role-Specific, Broad Scope	The SHRM BASK defines the **HR professional role in general**, not your specific job. You may encounter topics outside your current or past experience—study accordingly.
Global Applicability	For test-takers **outside the US**, US Employment Law content is replaced with other Workplace domain items. The BASK is designed for global relevance.
Use SHRM BASK for Personalized Study Plan	Break the BASK into segments to **identify strengths and gaps**. Review key concepts and proficiency indicators, and create a customized study guide. Use self-assessment questions to target areas for improvement.

Section 3

Using the SHRM BASK to Prepare for the SHRM-SCP Exam

In this section, we take what we learned in Section 2 and apply it to the HR Expertise areas and behavioral competencies, selecting an example of each to highlight how you can leverage the SHRM BASK in your test preparation. This process will help you figure out what you need to study to understand the nuance underlying the SHRM BASK.

HR Expertise Example: Structure of the HR Function

Using the recommended steps presented in Section 2, let's go through an example using the ***Structure of the HR Function*** knowledge area within the **Organization** knowledge domain. This technical knowledge area encompasses the people, processes and activities involved in the delivery of HR-related services that create and drive organizational effectiveness.

Note that the material presented under the HR Expertise technical competency will only be assessed with KIs.

Key Concepts

Because key concepts define testable content material, especially for KIs, we will start here and then move to proficiency indicators, selecting one example of each to examine more closely.

Step 1. Review Key Concepts

The first step is the most basic: Read the list of key concepts and the examples associated with the concepts. The key concepts for *Structure of the HR Function* are as follows:

» Approaches to HR function and service models.

» Approaches to HR structural models.

» Elements of the HR function.

» HR staff roles, responsibilities, and functions.

» Outsourcing of HR functions.

» HR-function metrics.

Step 2. Categorize Key Concepts According to Level of Familiarity

For each key concept, categorize them according to familiarity: extremely familiar, somewhat familiar (i.e., superficial knowledge), and limited to no familiarity. Make sure to review the associated examples as there may be some for which you may have more or less knowledge.

Step 3. Take Note of Any Key Concepts Requiring Additional Study

Any key concepts that fall into the latter two categories of somewhat or no familiarity are targets for further investigation and study. Identify these topics for your personal study guide. Recognize, of course, that a refresher review of any key concepts that you are already very comfortable with is a good idea to ensure your knowledge is up to date with the literature.

For this example, we will select the key concept—*elements of the HR function.*

- Examples of this key concept include *recruiting, talent management, compensation,* and *benefits.*

Step 4. Identify How the Key Concept May Be Assessed with a KI

When studying the various key concepts, it is easy to stick to learning the facts about the concept such as the details associated with a particular theory or the steps involved in a process. Think about how you might use your knowledge to demonstrate your understanding, and ability to solve situational problems, or predict outcomes.

Returning to our example, how might *elements of the HR function* be tested with a stand-alone KI?

To demonstrate how group dynamics can be assessed differently, Figures 3.1 and 3.2 present example KIs that reflect understanding and problem-solving, respectively.

Although both KI examples address elements of the HR function concepts, the recall item straightforwardly focuses on the definition of key terminology and does not require the test taker to do anything further than remember the information. The problem-solving KI, on the other hand, requires the test taker to take what they know about elements of the HR function and identify an effective solution to achieve the desired result of supporting the staffing of the new branch.

What is characterized by the measurement of employee behavior, employee turnover, and organizational performance?

A. Employee engagement

B. Career management

C. Job withdrawal

D. Performance management

Key: A, Employee Engagement

Description: This item requires the test taker to recall the definition of employee engagement to select the correct answer. Employee engagement is a measure of an individual's involvement in, satisfaction with, and enthusiasm for the work they are performing. A higher level of employee engagement has been shown in studies to affect customer satisfaction, company profit levels, employee turnover, and on-the-job accidents.

Figure 3.1. Recall KI for Elements of the HR Function

A department store chain is opening a new branch. The HR manager needs to hire 100 store assistants to start operations in three months. What is the best approach to ensure the store is appropriately staffed?

A. Engage the total rewards manager to work with recruiters for quick decisions on offers for successful candidates.

B. Assign HR team members to partner with line managers to lead recruiting and training locally at the new store.

C. Send the HR manager on a temporary assignment to manage the recruitment activities at the new store.

D. Meet with the VP of HR to discuss the risks associated with the compressed hiring timeline.

Key: B, Assign HR team members to partner with line managers to lead recruiting and training locally at the new store.

Description: This item is classified as problem-solving because it asks the test taker to assess the situation presented in the item and identify the best course of action given knowledge of elements of the HR function. Assigning an HR team member to partner with the line managers of the new branch is considered a best practice as it builds the local skillset to support future recruitment and training, while ensuring the ability to onboard a large number of new employees in a short amount of time.

Figure 3.2. Problem-Solving KI Elements for the HR Function

Proficiency Indicators

Proficiency indicators reflect HR best practices related to the HR technical competency or behavioral sub-competencies and can best be leveraged to identify context for situational prompts. As noted previously, they tend to be defined at the highest level of proficiency without dictating how the action can be accomplished. As a result, further analysis is required to support building a personal study guide.

Let's continue with our example of the functional knowledge area of *Structure of the HR Function* and apply the recommended process for one proficiency indicator.

Step 1. Review Proficiency Indicators for Advanced HR Professionals

For the SHRM-SCP exam, review the proficiency indicators listed for *Advanced HR Professionals*. The proficiency indicators for *Structure of the HR Function* are as follows:

» Designs, implements and adjusts the HR service model for the organization to ensure efficient and effective delivery of services to stakeholders.

» Creates long-term goals and implements changes that address feedback from stakeholders identifying opportunities for HR function improvements.

» Ensures that all elements of the HR function are aligned and integrated, and that they provide timely and consistent delivery of services to stakeholders.

- Identifies opportunities to improve HR operations by outsourcing work or implementing technologies that automate HR functions.
- Designs and oversees programs to collect, analyze and interpret HR-function metrics to evaluate the effectiveness of HR activities in supporting organizational success.

Step 2. Categorize Proficiency Indicators According to Level of Familiarity

For each proficiency indicator, ask yourself the following questions regarding your familiarity with them as a result of your HR career to date:

- Which indicators resonate with experiences I have had during my HR career? (Extremely Familiar)
- Which indicators am I only familiar with because I have observed others perform them? (Somewhat Familiar)
- Which indicators am I unfamiliar with altogether? (Limited to No Familiarity)

Categorize the indicators according to familiarity: extremely familiar, somewhat familiar (i.e., superficial knowledge), and limited to no familiarity.

Step 3. Take Note of Any Proficiency Indicators Requiring Additional Study

Take note of which proficiency indicators fall into each familiarity category. Unlike key concepts, they will all require further analysis to support your test preparation.

Step 4. Link Proficiency Indicators to Key Concepts

For each proficiency indicator, think about which key concepts are valuable for supporting the proficient performance of this proficiency indicator. Linking key concepts to proficiency indicators can aid your understanding of different applications for a key concept and scenarios you could encounter on the exam.

For example, let's look at the indicator, *ensures that all elements of the HR function are aligned and integrated, and that they provide timely and consistent delivery of services to stakeholders.* What key concepts are relevant to this indicator?

- *Approaches to HR function/service models* because understanding different approaches and service models is essential to ensuring that the approach supports timely and consistent delivery of services.
- *Approaches to HR structural models* because understanding these models is essential to ensuring the right model for the organization is in place.
- *Elements of the HR function* because these features are the foundation to the HR function.
- *HR staff roles, responsibilities and function* because understanding this concept will enable strategic allocation of resources to support effective service delivery.

The problem-solving KI example presented in Figure 3.2 effectively demonstrates how a proficiency indicator can be leveraged to identify a context for applying a key concept. For convenience, we re-present the stem with an explanation of the linkage in Figure 3.3.

Item Stem	Linkage Explanation
A department store chain is opening a new branch. The HR manager needs to hire 100 store assistants to start operations in three months. What is the best approach to ensure the store is appropriately staffed?	The item presents a situation and asks the test taker to recommend an approach to supporting the recruitment and onboarding of a large number of staff in a short period of time. This item requires knowledge of the key concept (*elements of the HR function*) and directly links to the proficiency indicator (*ensures that all elements of the HR function are aligned and integrated, and that they provide timely and consistent delivery of services to stakeholders*).

Figure 3.3. Key Concept Linkage Example: Technical Knowledge Area Proficiency Indicator

Step 5. Identify HR Best Practices

As written, there is a great deal of nuance in how a proficiency indicator can be accomplished or performed. Each proficiency indicator, as a result, can be broken down into lower-level components, each of which may have their own set of recommended best practices. Examining the lower-level steps or components will help you identify additional contextual situations that you may encounter on the exam, as well as additional key concepts that you may need to consider for review.

For each proficiency indicator

1. Think about how this proficiency indicator can be accomplished. What steps, factors, or other considerations are involved in satisfying the proficiency indicator?

   For this example indicator (*ensures that all elements of the HR function are aligned and integrated, and that they provide timely and consistent delivery of services to stakeholders*), factors to consider might include organizational and HR function metrics, feedback from stakeholders, outsourcing opportunities, workflow processes, or intended and unintended consequences to processes.

2. Identify any additional key concepts that you didn't initially select that could now be useful. Go back to the recommended steps for using key concepts to determine if these need to go on your study guide list.

   For example, if a lower-level step involves evaluating different service models to improve service delivery, you may want to add the key concept, *outsourcing of HR functions*, to your list of key concepts to study (if you haven't already).

3. Consider that you may know the ways that you have handled this proficiency indicator in the past and these responses may have been effective for your given situation, but they may not actually reflect HR best practices.

4. Take note of the situations you have encountered or witnessed that have involved this proficiency indicator as these could be reflected on the exam.

5. Identify and add any HR best practices and proficiency indicators to your study guide list as needed.

Behavioral Competency Example: Relationship Management

Now let's do the same thing using a behavioral competency as the starting point, using *Relationship Management* from the *Interpersonal* cluster. Relationship Management is defined as the KSAOs needed to create and maintain a network of professional contacts within and outside the organization, to build and maintain relationships, to work as an effective member of a team, and to manage conflict while supporting the organization.

As evident in Figure 2.2, key concepts are specified at the behavioral competency level. As a result, we will begin with the behavioral competency when reviewing key concepts and eventually narrow down to a sub-competency when examining the proficiency indicators.

Key Concepts

As we did for HR Expertise, we will present how to use the recommended approach, focusing on one key concept for demonstration.

Step 1. Review Key Concepts

Read the list of key concepts and the examples associated with the concepts. The key concepts for *Relationship Management* are as follows:

» Types of conflict.

» Conflict resolution strategies.

» Negotiation tactics, strategies, and styles.

» Trust-building techniques.

Step 2. Categorize Key Concepts According to Level of Familiarity

For each key concept, categorize them according to familiarity: extremely familiar, somewhat familiar (i.e., superficial knowledge), and limited to no familiarity. Make sure to review the associated examples as there may be some for which you may have more or less knowledge.

Step 3. Take Note of Any Key Concepts Requiring Additional Study

Any key concepts that fall into the latter two categories of somewhat or no familiarity are targets for further investigation and study. Identify these topics for your personal study guide. Recognize, of course, that a refresher review of any key concepts that you are already very comfortable with is a good idea to ensure your knowledge is up to date with the literature.

For this example, we will select the key concept of *conflict resolution strategies*. Examples of this key concept include accommodation, collaboration, compromise, competition, and avoidance.

Step 4. Identify How the Key Concept May Be Assessed with a KI

Think about how you might use your knowledge to demonstrate your understanding and ability to solve situational problems, or predict outcomes.

Returning to our example, how might *conflict resolution strategies* be tested with a standalone KI?

To demonstrate how conflict resolution strategies can be assessed differently, Figures 3.4 and 3.5 present examples of KIs that reflect understanding and problem-solving, respectively.

Although both KI examples address conflict resolution strategies and present example situations, the understanding item asks the test taker to assess the example and identify the term reflected in the example. The problem-solving KI, on the other hand, requires the test taker to take what they know about conflict resolution strategies and identify an effective solution to achieve the desired result of resolving the finance manager's frustrations.

Proficiency Indicators

Continuing with *Relationship Management*, let's look at the proficiency indicators and follow the recommended approach identified in Section 2. However, as noted previously, remember that proficiency indicators are specified under sub-competencies. For this exercise, we will focus on the sub-competency of *Conflict Management*, which focuses on the management and resolution of conflicts by identifying areas of common interest among the parties in conflict.

Which conflict-resolution style is most appropriate to find a temporary solution between groups who have opposite goals but equal power? A. Integrating B. Obliging C. Compromising D. Dominating	**Key**: C, Compromising **Description**: This item requires the test taker to use their knowledge of *conflict resolution strategies* and assess which style would achieve the desired result. The compromising resolution strategy focuses on finding a mutually agreeable solution that satisfies both parties and is considered the most effective to support an initial temporary solution until a more permanent solution can be achieved. Integrating strategy can also effectively bring both parties together but can be more time-consuming. The other two strategies balance the other party's needs against one's own and would not be effective for a temporary solution.

Figure 3.4. Understanding KI for Conflict Resolution Strategies

The finance manager expresses disappointment over a project that was launched by the HR department. Which approach should the HR manager take to resolve the finance manager's frustrations?

A. Discuss with the finance manager solutions or alternatives to the project.

B. Create a response to answer any questions about the benefits of the project.

C. Explain that in making the decision, the department was aware that not all employees would agree with the project.

D. Ask the finance manager to document suggestions for project improvements.

Key: A, Discuss with the finance manager solutions or alternatives to the project.

Description: This item requires that the test taker assess the situation presented and identify the best course of action given knowledge of *conflict resolution strategies*. Engaging in a discussion with the finance manager is considered an effective best practice because, unlike the other options, it involves a dialog and allows the HR manager to better understand the finance manager's issues to help reach a resolution.

Figure 3.5. Problem-Solving KI for Conflict Resolution Strategies

Step 1. Review Proficiency Indicators for Advanced HR Professionals

For the SHRM-SCP exam, review the proficiency indicators listed for *Advanced HR Professionals*. The proficiency indicators for *Conflict Management* are as follows:

» Designs and oversees conflict resolution strategies and processes throughout the organization.

» Facilitates difficult interactions among senior leaders to achieve optimal outcomes.

» Identifies and reduces potential sources of conflict when proposing new HR strategies or initiatives.

» Mediates or resolves escalated conflicts.

Step 2. Categorize Proficiency Indicators According to Level of Familiarity

For each proficiency indicator, ask yourself the following questions regarding your familiarity with them as a result of your HR career to date:

» Which indicators resonate with experiences I have had during my HR career? (Extremely Familiar)

» Which indicators am I only familiar with because I have observed others perform them? (Somewhat Familiar)

» Which indicators am I unfamiliar with altogether? (Limited to No Familiarity)

Categorize the indicators according to familiarity: extremely familiar, somewhat familiar (i.e., superficial knowledge), and limited to no familiarity.

Step 3. Take Note of Any Proficiency Indicators Requiring Additional Study

Take note of which proficiency indicators fall into each familiarity category. Unlike for key concepts, they will all require further analysis to support your test preparation.

Step 4. Link Proficiency Indicators to Key Concepts

For each proficiency indicator, think about which key concepts are valuable for supporting the proficient performance of this indicator. Linking key concepts to proficiency indicators can aid your understanding of different applications for a key concept and scenarios you could encounter on the exam.

For the indicator, *facilitates difficult interactions among senior leaders to achieve optimal outcomes*, for example, what key concepts are relevant to this indicator?

» *Types of conflict* because knowing the type of conflict may impact which strategies should be considered.

» *Conflict resolution strategies* because this indicator clearly focuses on designing processes in alignment with conflict resolution strategies.

» *Trust-building techniques* because effective conflict resolution typically involves employing the techniques presented as examples.

The problem-solving KI example presented in Figure 3.5 effectively demonstrates how a proficiency indicator can be leveraged to identify a context for applying a key concept. For convenience, we re-present the stem with an explanation of the linkage in Figure 3.6.

Behavioral sub-competency proficiency indicators can also provide situational context for SJIs. The next examples (Figure 3.7) showcase two SJIs based on the same scenario, both focusing on the sub-competency, Conflict Management.

Item Stem	Linkage Explanation
The finance manager expresses disappointment over a project that was launched by the HR department. Which approach should the HR manager take to resolve the finance manager's frustrations?	The item presents a situation and asks the test taker to recommend a conflict resolution approach to address the finance manager's frustration with a new HR initiative. This item requires knowledge of the key concept (conflict resolution strategies) and directly links to the proficiency indicator (facilitates difficult interactions among senior leaders to achieve optimal outcomes).

Figure 3.6. Key Concept Linkage Example: Sub-Competency Proficiency Indicator

SJI Scenario	
A manager approaches the HR director asking for assistance in resolving a conflict between two high-performing employees who report to the manager. One employee is less tenured, and the other employee has worked for the company for several years. The less-tenured employee complains that the long-tenured employee is very rude whenever he asks for information. As a result, this has made him unwilling to ask for assistance. The long-tenured employee, on the other hand, claims that the less-tenured employee is overreacting and that their relationship is fine. Meanwhile, clients have begun to complain about the two employees regarding a decrease in productivity, and a decline in customer service ratings. The manager has been unable to resolve the conflict and has asked the HR director to intervene.	
Conflict Management SJI 1	
Which action should the HR director take to resolve the conflict between the employees? A. Listen to each employee separately and suggest a solution to the manager. B. Partner with the manager to facilitate a mediation session between the employees. C. Require both employees to attend a conflict resolution training course. D. Meet with each employee separately to provide coaching on handling the situation.	**Key:** B, Partner with the manager to facilitate a mediation session between the employees.
Conflict Management SJI 2	
The HR director has noticed that conflicts between employees have been increasing across the company and that managers have been asking HR to intervene without actively trying to resolve the conflicts on their own. What should the HR director do to help managers handle employee conflicts? A. Send an email to all managers providing suggestions on resolving conflicts between employees. B. Create conflict resolution training for new managers entering the company. C. Provide conflict resolution training to all managers in the company. D. Require managers to document all steps they have taken before bringing an issue to HR.	**Key:** C, Provide conflict resolution training to all managers in the company.

Figure 3.7. SJIs for Conflict Management

Step 5. Identify HR Best Practices

This step is focused on doing a deeper dive into understanding the best practices associated with a proficiency indicator. Doing this analysis will help you identify additional contextual situations that you may encounter on the exam, as well as additional key concepts that you may need to consider for additional review.

For each proficiency indicator:

1. Think about how this proficiency can be accomplished. What steps, factors, or other considerations are involved in satisfying the proficiency indicator?

   For example, the indicator (designs and oversees conflict resolution strategies and processes throughout the organization) may involve considering factors such as organizational culture, existing policies and procedures, existing training and development opportunities, results from investigations, and stakeholder feedback.

2. Identify any additional key concepts that you didn't initially select that could now be useful. Go back to the recommended steps for using key concepts to determine if these need to go on your study guide list.

   For example, your initial review of the proficiency indicator may not have signaled that designing and overseeing conflict resolution strategies and processes throughout the organization could require negotiation tactics but now you do. Therefore, you may want to add the key concept (negotiation tactics, strategies, and styles) to your list of key concepts to study (if you haven't already).

3. Consider that you may know the ways that you have handled this proficiency indicator in the past and these responses may have been effective for your given situation, but they may not actually reflect HR best practices.

4. Take note of the situations you have encountered of witnessed that have involved this proficiency indicator as these could be reflected on the exam.

5. Identify and add any HR best practices and proficiency indicators to your study guide list, as needed.

Key Takeaway	Details & Guidance
Systematic Approach to Studying	Use a **structured process**: review key concepts and proficiency indicators for each HR Expertise area and behavioral competency. Categorize your familiarity (extremely, somewhat, limited/no knowledge) and target unfamiliar areas for deeper study.
Key Concepts Drive Knowledge Items	**Key concepts** are the foundation for Knowledge Items (KIs) on the exam. Understand definitions, examples, and how concepts may be tested at different cognitive levels (recall, understanding, problem-solving, critical evaluation).
Proficiency Indicators Link to Real-World Application	**Proficiency indicators** reflect HR best practices and are often assessed through situational prompts. Analyze each indicator for steps, factors, and best practices, and connect them to relevant key concepts.
Practice Linking Concepts and Indicators	For both technical and behavioral areas, practice **linking key concepts to proficiency indicators**. This helps you anticipate how exam questions may combine knowledge and practical scenarios.
Use Practice Items Strategically	Utilize **practice KIs and SJIs** to familiarize yourself with exam structure and question formats. However, do not rely solely on practice scores to predict exam success; use them to identify strengths and gaps.
Focus on HR Best Practices, Not Just Personal Experience	Reflect on how your own approaches compare to **industry best practices,** as outlined in the SHRM BASK. Your experience may not always align with exam expectations—study the recommended approaches.
Customize Your Study Guide	Build a **personalized study guide** by iteratively reviewing key concepts, proficiency indicators, and best practices. Add topics as you discover new connections or gaps, and adjust your plan based on ongoing self-assessment.

Section 4

The SHRM-SCP Exam Blueprint

Not only does SHRM provide the potential content areas for the SHRM-SCP exam in the SHRM BASK, SHRM also provides the actual breakdown of the numbers of exam items in the different content areas (Figure 4.1).

When measuring the three clusters of behavioral competencies, the exam includes close to equal representation from the different areas:

- **Leadership**: 19% of overall exam items.
- **Business**: 17.5% of overall exam items.
- **Interpersonal**: 13.5% of overall exam items.

In addition, for the HR knowledge domains, the People and Organization domains have more items than the Workplace domain. This difference is not surprising given the fact that Workplace only includes four functional areas, while People and Organization both include five functional areas.

- **People**: 19% of overall exam items.
- **Organization**: 18% of overall exam items.
- **Workplace**: 13% of overall exam items.

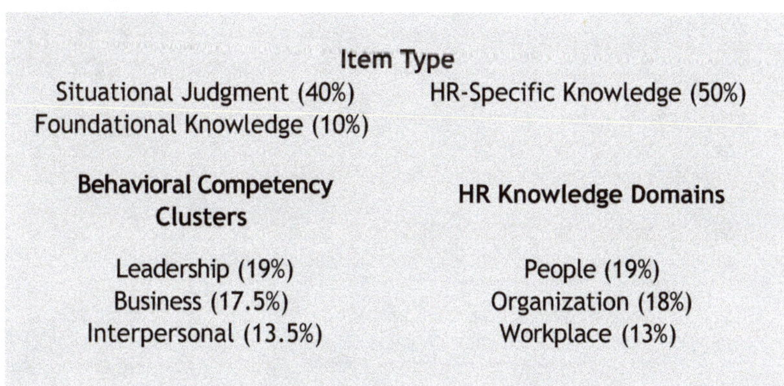

Item Type
Situational Judgment (40%)
HR-Specific Knowledge (50%)
Foundational Knowledge (10%)
Behavioral Competency Clusters
HR Knowledge Domains
Leadership (19%)
Business (17.5%)
Interpersonal (13.5%)
People (19%)
Organization (18%)
Workplace (13%)

Figure 4.1. Distribution of Exam Items by Content and Exam Type

Self-Assessment for Your Exam Study Plan

Now that you have seen and started interacting with the SHRM BASK, you might feel a bit overwhelmed by the sheer volume of potential exam content. In fact, many SHRM-SCP examinees are not sure what they should spend their time focused on and where they should start studying. Remember, the SHRM Certification Prep System is a robust option offering a comprehensive study package complete with pre-tests to assess your knowledge and identify gaps to provide a customized study plan based on your designated exam date.

To help diagnose your stronger and weaker areas and to direct your studying, we have put together this informal self-assessment for you. Note that this is not a true assessment of your knowledge but an informal resource you can use to determine where you need the most help and could benefit most in studying.

As you go through this assessment, try to be honest with yourself about your level of expertise. In many cases, you might not have a good understanding of your own knowledge level. That is okay and completely expected. If you are unsure of the meaning of terms, that is probably an indicator that you are not very knowledgeable in the area.

As a reminder, you can find the complete, complimentary, downloadable version of the SHRM BASK at:

https://www.shrm.org/credentials/certification/exam-preparation/bask

Instructions

Read the definition, sub-competencies (for behavioral competencies), key concepts, and proficiency indicators for all HR professionals. This will involve obtaining the full SHRM BASK and using the definitions and various pieces of information in it.

Rate the competencies and knowledge areas based on your level of expertise by placing an X in the appropriate box.

Section 1: Rate Competencies in Leadership Cluster

	Rate Your Level of Expertise		
	Low	Moderate	High
Leadership & Navigation			
Sub-competencies: » Navigating the organization » Vision » Managing HR initiatives » Influence			
Ethical Practice			
Sub-competencies: » Personal integrity » Professional integrity » Ethical agent			
Inclusive Mindset and Diversity (I&D)			
Sub-competencies: » Connecting I&D to Organizational Performance » Building the Infrastructure for an Inclusive and Diverse Culture » Ensuring Equity & Fairness » Cultivating an Inclusive and Diverse Culture » Operating in a Global Environment			

Section 2: Rate Competencies in Interpersonal Cluster

	Rate Your Level of Expertise		
	Low	Moderate	High
Relationship Management			
Sub-competencies: » Networking » Relationship building » Teamwork » Negotiation » Conflict management			
Communication			
Sub-competencies: » Delivering messages » Exchanging organizational information » Listening			

Section 3: Rate Competencies in Business Cluster

	Rate Your Level of Expertise		
	Low	**Moderate**	**High**
Business Acumen			
Sub-competencies: » Business and competitive awareness » Business analysis » Strategic alignment			
Consultation			
Sub-competencies: » Evaluating business challenges » Designing HR solutions » Advising on HR solutions » Change management » Service excellence			
Analytical Aptitude			
Sub-competencies: » Data advocate » Data gathering » Data analysis » Evidence-based decision-making			

Section 4: Rate Functional Areas in People Knowledge Domain

	Rate Your Level of Expertise		
	Low	**Moderate**	**High**
HR Strategy			
Talent Acquisition			
Employee Engagement & Retention			
Learning & Development			
Total Rewards			

Section 5: Rate Functional Areas in Organization Knowledge Domain

	Rate Your Level of Expertise		
	Low	**Moderate**	**High**
Structure of the HR Function			
Organizational Effectiveness & Development			
Workforce Management			
Employee & Labor Relations			
Technology Management			

Section 6: Rate Functional Areas in Workplace Knowledge Domain

	Rate Your Level of Expertise		
	Low	Moderate	High
Managing a Global Workforce			
Risk Management			
Corporate Social Responsibility			
US Employment Law & Regulations			

Scoring the Assessment

Based on your self-ratings of expertise for each behavioral competency or functional area, you can interpret the results based on your ratings of expertise.

Low Expertise = Study Most: These are areas where you have little to no expertise or experience. If you primarily support employee relations and employee engagement, you may need to study most in areas such as talent acquisition or inclusive mindset because you have little to no hands-on experience in this area.

Moderate Expertise = Study Some: These are areas where you have some expertise or experience, but you're not an expert. This could apply if you are a generalist with experience across many (or even most) competencies; you might have a surface-level knowledge of the competency, but you need to spend some time studying to better understand that competency outside of just your role or organization. If you used to work in a specific area but now perform a different set of job duties, this might apply too.

High Expertise = Review Only: These are the areas where you have the most expertise or experience. When you create your study plan, you don't want to spend too much time on these areas. Instead, you'll devote that time to studying the areas where you have more to learn. Note that these might be areas that you prefer to study or are most comfortable with. Because of this, you might have to fight the tendency to spend too much time in areas that you already know.

Interpreting the Assessment

You should now have 22 discrete ratings, one for each behavioral competency and functional area. Review your ratings and make notes about the terms, facts, and concepts that you need to learn or know more about so you can include them in your study plan.

It is important to review but not overstudy areas where your knowledge and familiarity with the content is already at a command-and-control level. Instead, focus your study efforts to improve your knowledge on the content with which you are least familiar. This means you should spend the majority of your study time on your study most areas, some time on your study some areas, and only a small amount of time on your review areas. Despite these recommendations, it is also important to note that the pass/fail decision for the exams are based on overall performance, rather than performance in each specific area. As a result, it is possible to pass the exam while performing rather poorly in a small number of subject areas.

After you have your completed self-assessment, group together the items on your checklist that you can study together to identify study blocks. As you sort items into groups, list the related terms and acronyms. After you've identified your study blocks, you'll have the outline for your study plan.

Also, we should note that the reference list at the end of the SHRM BASK has many relevant books and other resources that are relevant for learning more about these competencies and functional areas. Remember that it is not a comprehensive list, but these are resources that have been approved by SHRM for item writers to use when creating exam items.

Create a SMART Study Plan

A plan is when a *want to* becomes a *how to.*

After going through the self-assessment and gaining some understanding of the areas of the SHRM-SCP where you might need more studying, you should commit to making a plan for preparing for the exam. Although you might be able to follow a generic or informal plan, we know that the act of planning and committing is important for a lot of people to do things that are difficult.

One of the main reasons to focus on the study plan and schedule is the importance of writing things down. You are much more likely to take a commitment more seriously if you document it in a clear way. As such, we encourage you to take advantage of this workbook and use the templates provided in Appendix 2.

Here's how to create a study schedule that will fit into your life:[1]

1. Figure out how many hours you will need to cover everything on your study checklist. SHRM research shows that you should plan on spending at least 80 hours of preparation for the exam—although some people will need significantly more preparation time.

2. Start with the results of the self-assessment and plan your study time accordingly. You should also consider factors such as the extent of your HR experience and how quickly you tend to learn.

3. Determine how much of your time is already committed elsewhere. This will vary greatly between people. You should consider the time you need for family, work, exercise, personal care, and social activities, along with downtime and time for the unexpected, such as illness or a heavier-than-usual workload.

4. Decide how many hours of study time you will have available each week before the exam. If you plan to either form or join a study group or take an exam prep course, identify how many hours each week you will need for those activities. Then divide the remaining time into study sessions.

---

1 Charles Glover, eds., *Ace Your SHRM Certification Exam: The Official SHRM Study Guide for the SHRM-CP® and SHRM-SCP® Exams*, 4th ed. (London, Kogan Page)

5. Determine a specific, achievable goal for each study session and identify the content you will study so you can achieve that goal. Keep in mind that you'll need more study time for some content than for others and build time into your schedule for practice exams so that you can assess what you are learning.

6. Develop a realistic study schedule that shows your study sessions by date and time, the goal for each session, and the content you'll focus on during that session. Try to use this to make a realistic plan for an average of six to eight hours of study per week. Please note that there is no expectation of studying every day; however, it will be a good idea for you to plan on at least three days per week of some studying.

7. Create a week-by-week calendar that includes your scheduled activities for each day during your study period. Include time for family and friends, work (including your commute), scheduled appointments (doctors, dentists, etc.), exercise, and study sessions, study group meetings, and exam prep courses (if any).

Get Started on Your Study Schedule

Now step back and review your calendar:

- » How realistic is it?
- » Did you leave time for meals and personal care, as well as some downtime so you can rest and relax?
- » Did you leave buffer time in case of the unexpected?

If needed, go into your electronic calendar and set aside the time that you assigned to your studies.

Looking for next-level support in creating a study plan and sticking to it? As noted, the SHRM Certification Prep System will identify strengths and gaps in knowledge, allowing more time to prioritize the studying of weaker areas, and while maintaining your areas of strength.

A great feature in the SHRM Certification Prep System is the exam countdown calendar which will generate a customized study approach based on your selected exam date (and your proximity to it) top of mind, so you can plan your studies accordingly. You can pop in and out of the SHRM Certification Prep System when you have a little break, using your phone to access the many quizzes and lessons within the platform.

Key Takeaway	Details & Guidance
Exam Content Distribution is Defined	The SHRM-SCP exam provides a **clear breakdown of item distribution**: Leadership (19%), Business (17.5%), Interpersonal (13.5%), People (19%), Organization (18%), Workplace (13%). Use this to focus your study efforts proportionally.
Both Behavioral and Technical Domains are Covered	The exam **balances behavioral competencies** (Leadership, Business, Interpersonal) and **HR technical domains** (People, Organization, Workplace). Expect questions across all clusters and domains.
Self-Assessment Drives Effective Study Planning	Conduct a **self-assessment** for each competency and functional area, rating your expertise as Low, Moderate, or High. This helps you identify where to spend the most time studying.
Prioritize Study Time Based on Expertise	Allocate **most study time to Low expertise areas**, some to Moderate, and only review High expertise areas. Avoid overstudying familiar content—focus on gaps for maximum impact.
Group Related Topics for Efficient Learning	After self-assessment, **group related competencies and functional areas** into study blocks. This streamlines your study plan and helps reinforce connections between concepts.
Develop a SMART and Realistic Study Plan	Create a **SMART study plan** (Specific, Measurable, Achievable, Relevant, Time-bound). Schedule study sessions, set weekly goals, and include time for practice exams and review. Plan for 80+ hours of prep, adjusted to your needs.
Use SHRM Certification Prep System and Resources	Leverage the **SHRM Certification Prep System** for pre-tests, quizzes, and a customized countdown calendar. Use approved reference materials for deeper learning and ongoing progress tracking.

Section 5

The SHRM-SCP Twenty-Five-Item Practice Test

Introduction

This practice test includes 25 items that were previously used on the SHRM-SCP exam. These are different items than the ones that are used in the official SHRM study guide, *Ace Your SHRM Certification Exam*, and only include items from previous SHRM-SCP exams.

Similar to the real exam, this practice test is divided into separate sections that are composed of either knowledge items or situational judgment items.

» **Section 1** contains a total of 7 knowledge and foundational knowledge items.

» **Section 2** contains 10 situational judgment items.

» **Section 3** contains a set of 8 knowledge and foundational knowledge items.

Because this practice test only contains 25 items, it is not entirely representative of the entire blueprint that is used to build the SHRM-SCP exam. However, it is generally set up to cover all of the areas in the blueprint. This practice test will give you a taste of how the questions are structured on the exam and allow you to practice your test-taking strategies as you answer them.

To get a better sense of the real exams, SHRM recommends that you take the practice items during a timed period. We suggest you allot one and a half minutes per question (thirty-seven minutes total) to gauge your ability to answer questions under the time constraints of the real exams.

One very important caution: do not assume that the ability to answer items on this 25-item practice test directly correlates to a passing score on the certification exam. This practice test is composed of less than half of the number of items on the SHRM-SCP exam.

Additionally, the conditions in your at-home or in-office environment will not likely match the controlled environment in which a SHRM-SCP exam is administered. For these reasons, the practice items are intended to give a preview of the structure and format of test questions. It is not appropriate to use these results to predict an outcome on your exam, and doing well on the practice test is not a guarantee of a passing result on your exam.

Additional information, including the answer key and rationales for the correct answers for knowledge and foundational knowledge items, appear at the end of the practice test. Answer keys are also provided for the situational judgment items, but rationales are not provided due to the inherent nature of how these items are developed. Situational judgment items require judgment and decision-making to address workplace incidents, rather than relying on policy or law. All response options are actions that could be taken to respond to the situation, but there is only one *most effective* response. The most effective response is determined by diverse groups of experienced SHRM-certified HR professionals from around the globe who rate the effectiveness of each response. They also use the proficiency indicators outlined by the eight behavioral competencies in the SHRM BASK. Scoring the most effective response is only done if the group of HR experts agree that this is the best response of all given alternatives.

When answering the SJI questions, do not base your response on an approach that is specific to your organization. Rather, use your understanding of HR best practice, which is documented in the SHRM BASK, to select your response.

To further enhance your preparation for the exam, consider the SHRM Certification Prep System—which includes full-length SHRM-CP and SHRM-SCP practice (timed) exams full of previously used test items along with learning modules and over 2,700 practice items to help fill in your knowledge gaps. The SHRM Certification Prep System is offered in a variety of formats—self-study and virtual or in-person seminars—and through partner universities that are authorized to teach the SHRM Certification Prep System content.

If you would like additional confidence that you are selecting the right exam level, SHRM Certification Previews offer unique quizzes complete with retired SHRM exam questions. These mobile-friendly exam previews are designed to enhance your exam readiness in conjunction with the SHRM Learning System, to aid you with the following options:

- **"Pick the Right Exam for You":** Identifying which of the SHRM exams is right for you, with offerings complete with SHRM-CP and SHRM-SCP questions,

- **Half-length Quizzes:** Sixty-seven question quizzes half the length of the which cover the full range of the SHRM BASK pertaining to either the SHRM-CP or SHRM-SCP, respectively.

- **Domain-level Offerings:** Question sets dedicated solely to the individual HR Functional Areas: Workplace, Organization, People, or the Behavioral Clusters: Interpersonal, Business, Leadership, offering you a deep dive into one of the six content domains..

- **Item Type Offerings:** If you are looking to practice SJIs specifically, or KIs, we offer quizzes dedicated solely to those specific item types, covering a diverse range of content areas..

SHRM-SCP Practice Test Questions

Section 1: This section is composed of seven (7) knowledge items.

1. Implementing sustainable corporate social responsibility initiatives results in which internal positive impact?

   A. Improves employee morale.

   B. Attracts new investors.

   C. Presents opportunities to grow the business.

   D. Reflects the company's core values.

2. Which communication medium is most appropriate for an HR manager to initially inform an employee that the employee's position has been discontinued?

   A. Phone call

   B. Email

   C. In person

   D. Formal letter

3. A CEO is concerned about an escalated rate of employee turnover and believes it is due to poor leadership by department managers. Which approach should the HR manager suggest to evaluate the CEO's belief about leadership?

   A. Train department managers on effective leadership techniques.

   B. Conduct a performance analysis for the leadership team.

   C. Solicit employee perceptions of their department managers.

   D. Ask department managers for their opinions on the cause of high turnover.

4. A team wants to internally develop project management soft skills or abilities among its members while completing their project. Which approach best accomplishes this goal?

   A. Utilizing a mentoring approach for less-experienced team members.

   B. Paying a project completion bonus for all project team members.

   C. Creating a cross-functional team so all organizational needs are met.

   D. Changing the leadership of the project team.

5. Which is the first step the HR manager should take when planning to negotiate a resolution to a workplace investigation?

   A. Set clear objectives for achieving desired results.

   B. Understand the parties involved and their expectations.

   C. Develop options by anticipating what others may accept.

   D. Prepare for objections with responses to anticipated questions.

6. Self-paced courses share advantages and disadvantages of which approach to training and development?

   A. Classroom

   B. On-the-job

   C. Simulations

   D. Distance learning

7. After completing an 18-month onboarding process to adjust to the organization's culture, new hires are encouraged to reflect on their work. Which type of culture is this company exhibiting?

   A. Learning

   B. Performing

   C. Participating

   D. Growing

Section 2: This section has ten (10) situational judgment items (SJIs).

The following scenario accompanies the next two items.

A company hires external consultants to conduct one-on-one sessions with employees to discuss recent declines in overall company morale. During the sessions, the consultants encourage employees to share concerns about the company and the leadership team. They also request employee opinions on successes and failures regarding company operations and strategy. Employees do not sign confidentiality agreements but are told the sessions are recorded and their feedback will remain anonymous in any reports to leadership. After the sessions, the HR manager learns that the consultants were pressured by the leadership team to provide copies of the recordings. Some of the recordings were reviewed by the leadership team in the presence of several managers. The entire company is now aware of the breach of confidentiality. Several employees voice their concerns to the HR manager because they are afraid of retaliation.

8. Several months after the incident, employee morale reaches its lowest in company history. Which action should the HR manager take first to address this issue?

   A. Train managers on effective ways to regularly engage with their employees.

   B. Recommend increasing employee compensation and bonuses.

   C. Conduct focus groups with employees to identify ways the company can regain their trust.

   D. Review exit interview data to gain a better understanding of employee exit decisions.

9. Which action should the HR manager take first to mitigate the impact of the information release on organizational trust?

   A. Issue a legal notice to the consultants for violating the anonymity of the meetings.

   B. Recommend the leadership team issue an apology to all employees to guarantee no retaliation.

   C. Ask the consultants to attend a companywide meeting to explain why the release happened.

   D. Require the employees who heard the recordings to sign a confidentiality agreement.

The following scenario accompanies the next three items.

A nonprofit organization operates a facility that provides social services, including housing, food, job placement, and health care. Most services are performed by entry-level employees, who make up 60% of the staff. Entry-level employees report to the facility manager, who assigns them to various positions depending on daily staffing needs. Over the past 12 months, turnover among entry-level employees has increased, and it has become increasingly difficult to attract and retain employees in these positions. The average tenure for an entry-level employee has decreased to six months. The organization provides a competitive benefits package, but base pay for all employees is lower than the market average. Many entry-level employees work extra shifts to cover staffing shortages and earn overtime pay. Additionally, entry-level employees must complete quarterly skills training courses within their first year of employment, which a third-party vendor supports. The company pays for all training courses upfront, resulting in financial loss each time an employee leaves the company before completing the training. After assessing exit interview data and interviewing incumbent employees, the HR director believes that base pay is a leading factor in employee turnover. The HR director believes the organization must change its strategies to remain competitive.

10. The facility manager notifies the HR director that entry-level employees are starting to show symptoms of burnout due to overwork. Which approach should the HR director take to address employee workload?

    A. Distribute pamphlets that provide information on the organization's employee support resources.

    B. Announce to employees that overtime for entry-level employees will be limited.

    C. Host a town hall meeting to discuss the organization's need for increased staffing.

    D. Work with the facility manager to develop a staffing schedule to ensure work is equally distributed.

11. The HR director is preparing a business case for leadership to support the need to increase base pay for entry-level employees. Which action should the HR director take first?

    A. Examine compensation strategies used by nonprofit organizations in the local region that provide similar services.

    B. Calculate the cost of increasing the base pay of entry-level employees up to the market average for the organization.

    C. Develop a step-rate pay structure for entry-level employees to be eligible for pay increases after one year with the organization.

    D. Determine how well the proposed increases fit within the current budget.

12. Which action should the HR director take to reduce the organization's entry-level employee training-related losses?

    A. Direct the facility manager to develop an internal training program to eliminate the need for third-party skills training.

    B. Modify the organization's recruiting strategy to attract candidates with experience in the field.

    C. Partner with the third-party vendor to consolidate the delivery of the courses to twice per year.

    D. Establish a peer training program for senior employees to train entry-level employees.

The following scenario accompanies the next two items.

A large multinational manufacturing company holds an annual meeting with its regional HR leaders and company leadership, including the HR VP. During the meeting, a regional HR leader disagrees with the CEO about the company's priorities for the HR leader's region. The regional HR leader believes the high turnover in the region is caused by low employee morale, while the CEO believes it is due to external economic factors. The regional HR leader wants to focus on hiring high-performing employees and improving employee morale, and the CEO wants the regional HR leader to focus on hiring as many factory employees as possible. The disagreement escalates, and the CEO and regional HR leader continue to argue for several minutes.

13. The CEO asks the HR VP to provide an opinion. How should the HR VP respond to try to resolve the disagreement?

    A. Ask the CEO to put off this discussion until later in the day when both parties have had more time to think about the issue.

    B. Tell the HR leader that the CEO is leading the company's strategic direction so the HR leader should focus on the CEO's priorities.

    C. Remind the CEO that the HR leader has a better perspective of the local region's needs.

    D. Suggest the HR leader create a business case to present to the CEO at a later date.

14. The regional HR leader says employee morale is low because some factory positions have been replaced by automation. This has increased safety but decreased the salaries of employees who have had to change positions. The regional HR leader asks the HR VP how the company plans to improve morale. How should the HR VP respond?

A. Offer to send monthly updates to employees explaining the beneficial aspects of automation.

B. Recommend the regional HR leader give pay raises to front-line employees whose salaries were cut.

C. Suggest putting a temporary freeze on implementing any further automation.

D. Recommend the regional HR leader hold a meeting with employees to discuss concerns.

The following scenario accompanies the next three items.

The HR director for a hotel chain is copied on an email from the CFO notifying all hotel staff to start giving guests a pamphlet for a specific religion with their room keys at check-in. According to the CFO, the pamphlets will arrive tomorrow, and staff should begin distributing them immediately. The HR director knows that distributing religious pamphlets conflicts with the hotel chain's brand standards and core values related to inclusion and diversity for employees and customers. Several site HR managers notify the HR director that onsite hotel staff are threatening to quit if they are required to distribute the pamphlets. It has been challenging to fill open hotel staff positions for the last year due to a limited number of job applicants, so the HR director anticipates that backfilling vacant hotel staff roles will not happen quickly. Additionally, the HR director is notified that the chain's customer service team has started receiving guest complaints about a hotel manager's social media post, which praises the hotel chain's leadership team for upholding a specific religion's values. The manager's post violates the hotel chain's social media policy, which states that employees may not speak on behalf of the company on any platform.

15. The hotel manager agrees to take down the social media post. How should the HR director address the hotel manager's violation of the hotel chain's social media policy?

A. Block staff members from using social media while connected to the hotel's Internet.

B. Discuss with the hotel manager how expressing preferential statements impacts the workplace.

C. Encourage hotel employees to share feedback with the hotel manager about the impact of the post.

D. Ask the hotel manager to post an apology for the previous social media post.

16. How should the HR director explain to the CFO why the decision to distribute religious pamphlets is a violation of brand standards and core values?

    A. Emphasize the potential public relations repercussions to the CFO based on the online customer complaints.

    B. Present the CFO a report outlining potential financial repercussions the hotel chain might experience from losing hotel staff.

    C. Explain to the CFO how the instruction to distribute the pamphlets contradicts the hotel chain's core values.

    D. Share metrics with the CFO demonstrating the diverse religious makeup of cities where the chain's hotels are located.

17. Several hotel staff refuse to come to work the next day if they are required to distribute the pamphlets. Which action should the HR director take first to address their concerns?

    A. Tell hotel staff to avoid distributing the pamphlets until further notice from HR.

    B. Notify hotel staff that distributing the pamphlets is not mandatory.

    C. Ask hotel managers to prepare a plan for working with reduced staff.

    D. Inform hotel staff that paid time off may be used if they intend to miss work.

Section 3: This section is composed of eight (8) knowledge items.

18. Which competencies in the Ulrich model are critical for HR business partners and strategic advisors to promote organizational agility?

    A. Compensation and business acumen.

    B. Subject matter knowledge and ability.

    C. Change and paradox navigation.

    D. Security and employee assistance.

19. What is the primary purpose of creating job offers contingent upon the results of a background check?

    A. Ensures that no one with a criminal history has access to sensitive information.

    B. Protects against negligent hiring while allowing candidates to compete fairly.

    C. Reduces the organization's insurance costs through responsible hiring.

    D. Safeguards the company from being accused of employee poaching.

20. An HR manager wants to understand employees' opinions on a new benefits program. Which type of data collection method will be most effective?

    A. Surveys

    B. Interviews

    C. Observations

    D. Focus groups

21. How does an automated audit process assist with benefits management?

    A. Reconciling errors on invoices.

    B. Processing claims inquiries.

    C. Analyzing plans' market competitiveness.

    D. Forecasting new enrollment fees.

22. Which two factors help determine the likelihood of an international candidate adjusting well and succeeding in another country?

    A. The candidate's cultural adaptability and any accompanying family members' support.

    B. The seniority of the role and an increase in compensation that raises the candidate's standard of living.

    C. An agreement on the return date to the home country and a generous personal travel allowance.

    D. The ability to remain abroad if desired and have pleasant and productive colleagues with whom to collaborate.

23. Which is the first step in establishing a pipeline of talented employees?

    A. Develop plans to recruit talented potential employees from external sources.

    B. Create an internal career planning process for existing talented employees.

    C. Increase the engagement level of talented employees through special assignments.

    D. Understand business strategy to support future demand for talented employees.

24. Which term describes how much risk a company is willing to take stated in quantitative or qualitative terms?

    A. Risk assessment.

    B. Risk appetite.

    C. Risk response.

    D. Risk indicator.

25. Which practice is an acceptable labor practice by an employer during the election of a bargaining unit?

    A. Communicating with employees to understand their reasons for remaining nonunionized.

    B. Promising benefits to employees contingent upon rejection of the union.

    C. Questioning the employees about their perception of the union's performance.

    D. Conducting an open ballot to determine how many employees support the union.

Appendix 1

The SHRM-SCP Practice Test Answers

Question Number	Item Data		Rationale
1	Domain	WORKPLACE	"Improves employee morale" is correct. This is the correct answer because sustaining CSR results in a huge impact on the internal organization.
	Sub-competency	CORPORATE SOCIAL RESPONSIBILITY	
	Difficulty	Somewhat Hard	
	Key	A	
2	Domain	INTERPERSONAL	"In person" is correct. This is correct because this allows the person conducting the termination to properly show empathy and support for the employee, allows for the employee to sign and/or receive any documents, and allows for the employee to collect their personal belongings.
	Sub-competency	COMMUNICATION	
	Difficulty	Easy	
	Key	C	
3	Domain	BUSINESS	"Conduct a performance analysis" is correct. When diagnosing the causes of poor performance, it is important to consider whether the poor performance is detrimental to the business. That is, is poor performance critical to completing the job, and does it affect business results? If it is detrimental, then the next step is to conduct a performance analysis to determine the cause of poor performance.
	Sub-competency	ANALYTICAL APTITUDE	
	Difficulty	Somewhat Hard	
	Key	B	
4	Domain	PEOPLE	"Utilizing a mentoring approach..." is correct. Having mentors share their expertise with others on the team will expose those with less experience to more skills and processes, furthering their skill development.
	Sub-competency	HR STRATEGY	
	Difficulty	Somewhat Easy	
	Key	A	
5	Domain	ORGANIZATION	"Understand the parties..." is correct. This is correct because knowing what each party expects is the first step to setting the stage in planning a negotiation.
	Sub-competency	EMPLOYEE & LABOR RELATIONS	
	Difficulty	Somewhat Hard	
	Key	B	

Question Number	Item Data		Rationale
6	Domain	PEOPLE	"Distance learning" is correct. Since self-directed learning is a form of distance or e-learning, they share the same advantages and disadvantages.
	Sub-competency	LEARNING & DEVELOPMENT	
	Difficulty	Easy	
	Key	D	
7	Domain	PEOPLE	"Learning" is correct. This is correct because in a learning organization, the employees are repeatedly encouraged to reflect on what they learn, to apply it to their work, and then pass it along to others.
	Sub-competency	EMPLOYEE ENGAGEMENT & RETENTION	
	Difficulty	Somewhat Hard	
	Key	A	
8	Domain	BUSINESS	Situational judgment items (SJIs) require the examinee to think about what is occurring in the scenario and decide which response option identifies the most effective course of action. Other response options may be something you could do to respond in the situation, but SJIs require thinking and acting based on the best of the available options. Do not base your answer on your organization's approach to handling the situation but, rather, answer based on what you know should be done according to best practice. Panels of SHRM-certified subject matter experts rate the effectiveness of each response option, and the "best" answer is derived by statistical analysis of those expert opinions.
	Sub-competency	CONSULTATION	
	Difficulty	Easy	
	Key	C	
9	Domain	LEADERSHIP	
	Sub-competency	ETHICAL PRACTICE	
	Difficulty	Somewhat Easy	
	Key	B	
10	Domain	BUSINESS	
	Sub-competency	CONSULTATION	
	Difficulty	Easy	
	Key	D	
11	Domain	BUSINESS	
	Sub-competency	ANALYTICAL APTITUDE	
	Difficulty	Hard	
	Key	B	
12	Domain	BUSINESS	
	Sub-competency	CONSULTATION	
	Difficulty	Somewhat Hard	
	Key	D	

Question Number	Item Data		Rationale
13	Domain	INTERPERSONAL	
	Sub-competency	RELATIONSHIP MANAGEMENT	
	Difficulty	Somewhat Easy	
	Key	D	
14	Domain	LEADERSHIP	
	Sub-competency	LEADERSHIP & NAVIGATION	
	Difficulty	Somewhat Easy	
	Key	D	
15	Domain	LEADERSHIP	
	Sub-competency	INCLUSIVE MINDSET	
	Difficulty	Easy	
	Key	B	
16	Domain	INTERPERSONAL	
	Sub-competency	COMMUNICATION	
	Difficulty	Easy	
	Key	C	
17	Domain	LEADERSHIP	
	Sub-competency	INCLUSIVE MINDSET	
	Difficulty	Somewhat Easy	
	Key	A	
18	Domain	ORGANIZATION	"Change and paradox navigation" is correct. These are two of the competencies most critical to his model of being a strong business partner and having the ability to drive the organization to think through alignments that would positively impact its execution of strategy, and generally need to be an ambassador of change. Thinking through different business challenges, this role helps leaders get past ambiguity and come up with solutions
	Sub-competency	STRUCTURE OF THE HR FUNCTION	
	Difficulty	Hard	
	Key	C	
19	Domain	PEOPLE	"Protects against negligent hiring..." is correct. This is correct because waiting to conduct a background check until the offer is made ensures all candidates are able to compete for the job without bias while providing the organization with an opportunity to ensure they are not knowingly risking the safety of others.
	Sub-competency	TALENT ACQUISITION	
	Difficulty	Easy	
	Key	B	

Question Number	Item Data		Rationale
20	Domain	BUSINESS	"Survey" is correct. This is correct because pulse surveys are specifically designed to gather impressions on certain topics.
	Sub-competency	ANALYTICAL APTITUDE	
	Difficulty	Somewhat Easy	
	Key	A	
21	Domain	ORGANIZATION	"Reconciling errors on invoices" is correct. Manual reconciliations do not catch as many invoice errors as an automated audit process. These can compare the billing data to identify discrepancies across applications and systems.
	Sub-competency	TECHNOLOGY MANAGEMENT	
	Difficulty	Somewhat Hard	
	Key	A	
22	Domain	WORKPLACE	"The candidate's cultural adaptability..." is correct. Certain personality traits, such as extroversion, openness to new experiences, and agreeableness, have been shown to increase the likelihood that the expat will complete the assignment. The same is true for their family members.
	Sub-competency	MANAGING A GLOBAL WORKFORCE	
	Difficulty	Easy	
	Key	A	
23	Domain	ORGANIZATION	"Understand business strategy..." is correct. In order to plan for future needs, an understanding of the business strategy and plans is the essential first step.
	Sub-competency	WORKFORCE MANAGEMENT	
	Difficulty	Easy	
	Key	D	
24	Domain	WORKPLACE	"Risk appetite" is correct. Risk appetite is a measure of how much risk a company is willing to take.
	Sub-competency	RISK MANAGEMENT	
	Difficulty	Somewhat Easy	
	Key	B	
25	Domain	WORKPLACE	"Communicating with employees..." is correct. Employers can communicate without threatening, interrogating, promising, or spying on employees concerning union creation.
	Sub-competency	US EMPLOYMENT LAW & REGULATIONS	
	Difficulty	Somewhat Hard	
	Key	A	

Appendix 2

Twelve-Week Study Schedule Template

We have provided a set of study schedule templates to guide your SHRM-SCP exam preparation. Please use these spaces to create your plan and write it down.

Planned Test Date with Prometric: ____________________

Study Week 1: ____________________

Weekly Goal: This week, I will...

____

____

____

____

	Planned Time	Study Focus
Sunday		
Monday		
Tuesday		
Wednesday		
Thursday		
Friday		
Saturday		

Study Week 2: ____________________

Weekly Goal: This week, I will...

____

____

____

____

	Planned Time	Study Focus
Sunday		
Monday		
Tuesday		
Wednesday		
Thursday		
Friday		
Saturday		

Study Week 3: ________________

Weekly Goal: This week, I will...

____

____

____

____

	Planned Time	Study Focus
Sunday		
Monday		
Tuesday		
Wednesday		
Thursday		
Friday		
Saturday		

Study Week 4: ________________

Weekly Goal: This week, I will...

	Planned Time	Study Focus
Sunday		
Monday		
Tuesday		
Wednesday		
Thursday		
Friday		
Saturday		

Study Week 5: ________________

Weekly Goal: This week, I will...

____

____

____

____

	Planned Time	Study Focus
Sunday		
Monday		
Tuesday		
Wednesday		
Thursday		
Friday		
Saturday		

Study Week 6: ________________

Weekly Goal: This week, I will...

____

____

____

____

	Planned Time	Study Focus
Sunday		
Monday		
Tuesday		
Wednesday		
Thursday		
Friday		
Saturday		

Study Week 7: ________________

Weekly Goal: This week, I will...

____

____

____

____

	Planned Time	Study Focus
Sunday		
Monday		
Tuesday		
Wednesday		
Thursday		
Friday		
Saturday		

Study Week 8: ________________

Weekly Goal: This week, I will...

____

____

____

____

	Planned Time	Study Focus
Sunday		
Monday		
Tuesday		
Wednesday		
Thursday		
Friday		
Saturday		

Study Week 9: ________________

Weekly Goal: This week, I will...

____

____

____

____

	Planned Time	Study Focus
Sunday		
Monday		
Tuesday		
Wednesday		
Thursday		
Friday		
Saturday		

Study Week 10: ________________

Weekly Goal: This week, I will...

____

____

____

____

	Planned Time	Study Focus
Sunday		
Monday		
Tuesday		
Wednesday		
Thursday		
Friday		
Saturday		

Study Week 11: ________________

Weekly Goal: This week, I will...

____

____

____

____

	Planned Time	Study Focus
Sunday		
Monday		
Tuesday		
Wednesday		
Thursday		
Friday		
Saturday		

Study Week 12: ________________

Weekly Goal: This week, I will...

___

___

___

___

	Planned Time	Study Focus
Sunday		
Monday		
Tuesday		
Wednesday		
Thursday		
Friday		
Saturday		

Index

Looking for another book?

Explore our award-winning books from global business experts in Human Resources, Learning and Development

Scan the code to browse

www.koganpage.com/hr-learning-development

Ace Your SHRM Certification Exam

The Official SHRM Study Guide for the SHRM-CP® and SHRM-SCP® Exams

Plus 50 SHRM-CP and SHRM-SCP Practice Items

ISBN: 9781398627734

www.koganpage.com

From 4 December 2025 the EU Responsible Person (GPSR) is:
eucomply oÜ, Pärnu mnt. 139b – 14, 11317 Tallinn, Estonia
www.eucompliancepartner.com

www.ingramcontent.com/pod-product-compliance
Lightning Source LLC
Chambersburg PA
CBHW081202020426
42333CB00020B/2602

* 9 7 8 1 3 9 8 6 2 7 7 9 6 *